HENK VAN OORT, a primary teacher by degree in English at the Amsterdam University. He has taught for more than 40 years in primary and secondary education, including class teaching in a Steiner school, teaching English, and running educational courses and seminars for teachers and parents. His interest in literature and poetry has led to his appearance at storytelling and poetry seminars, and his introductory courses to anthroposophy are highly successful. Based in Bergen N.H. in the Netherlands, Henk van Oort is married and the father of three grown-up children. He is the author of *Anthroposophy, A Concise Introduction* and *A–Z Anthroposophy*.

The Inner Rainbow

*An illustrated history of human consciousness
from Ancient India to the present day*

Henk van Oort

TEMPLE LODGE

First published in Great Britain in 2014 by Temple Lodge Publishing,
Hillside House, The Square
Forest Row, RH18 5ES

E-mail: office@templelodge.com

www.templelodge.com

© Henk van Oort 2014

All rights reserved. Apart from any fair dealing for the purpose of private study, research, criticism or review, as permitted under the Copyright, Designs and Patents Act, 1988, no part of this publication may be reproduced, stored in a retrieval system, or transmitted in any form or by any means, electronic, electrical, chemical, mechanical, optical, photocopying, recording or otherwise, without the prior written permission of the copyright owner. Inquiries should be addressed to the Publishers

Painting of The Green Snake and the Beautiful Lily by David Newbatt reproduced by kind permission. Other image sources: public domain, commons and the author's collection. Every effort has been made to identify copyright holders. The publishers will be happy to correct any ommisions in future editions

A catalogue record for this book is available from the British Library

ISBN 978 1 906999 60 5

Cover by Morgan Creative
Typeset by DP Photosetting, Neath, West Glamorgan
Printed and bound by Beforts Ltd., Hertfordshire

Contents

Acknowledgements	vii
Introduction	1
Prologue: The Rainbow	7

Ancient India
Krishna and Arjuna	9

Ancient Persia
Ahura Mazda and Zarathustra	11
Avesta	13

Ancient Egypt and Babylonia
Ziggurat	14
The Tower of Babel	15
Gilgamesh	17
The Pyramids	19
The Obelisk	21
The Erected Stone	23
Tutankhamun	25
David	27

Ancient Greece
The Golden Bough	29
Ulysses and the Cyclops	31
The Minotaur	33
King Aegeus at Delphi	35
Achilles Tries to Kill Agamemnon	37
Olympia	38
Plato's Cave	40
The Mission of Wine	42
Metre and Memory Systems	45

Ancient Rome
The Colosseum	48
St Augustine	50

Germanic Mythology
  Yggdrasil   52

The Middle Ages
  Chartres   54

Early Renaissance
  Mont Ventoux   56
  Perspective   59

Sixteenth Century
  Memory Theatre   62
  Copernicus   64
  Hans Holbein   66

Seventeenth Century
  Rembrandt   68
  Still-life Painting   72
  Isaac Newton   74

Eighteenth Century
  A Scientific Experiment   76
  Coalbrookdale By Night   78
  Robinson Crusoe   80
  The Feast of Reason   83
  William Blake   87

Modern Times
  Rudolf Steiner   89
  Heralds of the World Wide Web   91
  The First Argonne Computer   94
  The Sputnik   96
  Google   98

Epilogue   100

Further Reading   104

Acknowledgements

I would like to thank the late Ms Lena Struik, the Waldorf teacher in my village, who once met Rudolf Steiner during one of his lectures in Holland and who introduced me to Rudolf Steiner's *World History in the Light of Anthroposophy*. This series of lectures, given in Dornach in 1923/24, is the ultimate source of inspiration for this book.

Introduction

Whenever the concept of history is discussed we seem to concentrate on an almost infinite sequence of events that took place in the past. It is generally accepted that life on earth was different in ancient times. We realize that all sorts of inventions had not yet been made and that people back then had a limited view of their geographical position on planet earth. Time was, we are told, more a circular phenomenon than the modern linear concept we have nowadays. Many more aspects of the concept of history could be summed up, but hardly ever the aspect of changing consciousness is mentioned or dealt with at any depth. Through all preceding centuries the power of thought of the human phenomenon radically and irreversibly changed again and again. This ongoing change of consciousness is the subject of this book. From more or less generally known highlights taken from the history of art and from literature I have tried to demonstrate that human consciousness has definitely changed over the ages. From carefully observing pictorial and poetic expression brought forth by the consecutive cultural periods we can conclude that the way in which people saw themselves and their surroundings was liable to continuous transformation. The question arises where such an extensive overview of this transformational process should start. I have chosen to more or less follow Rudolf Steiner's classification of those cultural periods which have contributed to the present state of what is now known as 'western civilization'. That does not mean that other civilizations, the ones that are not mentioned in this overview, are of less value. These have been left out because they only indirectly influenced the formative process that is described in this book. It has been a matter of choice and, of course, space is limited in this publication.

The journey through time described in this book starts in a vague and somewhat mysterious past. It is the watershed moment at which the legendary continent of Atlantis sank into the Atlantic Ocean around 10,000 years BC. Plato tells us in his *Timaeus* and in his *Critias* that Manu led a group of people away from the disaster to safer regions. Finally these people arrived in present India where the Ancient Indian cultural period started under the star sign of Cancer in 7227 BC and lasted till 5067 BC. The cultural periods are linked to the characteristics and influences of the signs of the zodiac. The cultural periods last approximately 2160 years each, which is the timespan in which the vernal point, the point where the sun rises in spring, travels from a given sign of the zodiac to the following one.

The torch of this transformational process was handed over to the second post-Atlantean culture, Ancient Persia, which lasted from 5067 till 2907 BC, under the star sign Gemini. The civilization of Ancient India of course did not cease to exist but it turned into a less influential strain in the development of human consciousness. Again the transformational process of human consciousness was taken over, this time by two civilizations simultaneously. The third post-Atlantean cultural period was given shape by Ancient Egypt and Ancient Babylonia—2907 till 747 BC, star sign Taurus. After the heyday of these two important civilizations the torch was handed over to ancient Greece and ancient Rome, not specifically at the same time but more or less the one after the other—747 BC till AD 1413, star sign Aries. The present fifth post-Atlantean cultural period has not been given a special name by Rudolf Steiner. It will last from 1413 till AD 3573, under the star sign Pisces. These five periods will be followed by two more: the Russian cultural period AD 3573–5733, star sign Aquarius, and the American cultural period, AD 5733–7893, star sign Capricorn. What can be said of the ensuing development lies beyond the scope of this book.

The connecting thread that ties in these cultural periods, each contributing to the development of human consciousness in their own way, is the creation and further maturation of the human 'I'. I do not use the word 'ego' in this context. 'Ego' can be translated as 'from the earth' (E = from, Go = Gaea = Earth), in other words the lower self. The 'I' is the higher self, the entity that does not die and travels from incarnation to incarnation. The 'I' and human consciousness are inextricably linked. The 'I' did not exist as an independent sheath of the human being at the start of the Ancient Indian cultural period. Correspondingly it can be said that human consciousness was not an individualized phenomenon. The capacity of saying 'I' to oneself was not there. Human beings back then did not experience themselves as self-conscious, independent beings as we do now. On the contrary, human beings felt themselves one with the world of the spirit. They were led and inspired by their leaders, who could be priests, prophets, pharaohs, kings. With their enhanced power of perception these initiates as intermediaries were inspired by their Gods and acted as a group-'I' giving directives and instructions when establishing and maintaining a civilization.

The purpose of the evolution of humanity consists in man becoming more and more involved in the physical existence on earth. In the Ancient Indian cultural period man felt completely at home in the spiritual world. This implied at the same time that he experienced his daily life on earth in a partially dreamlike way. He did not take full possession of his body when he awoke in the morning as we do today. He did not wake up into the same physical consciousness as is the case in our present state of development. As a remnant from ancient Atlantean times to him the objects did not have the same clear-cut outlines as we have today because human beings were still clairvoyant. The aura of living beings could be seen by everyone, not just by the initiates. The task of the initiates was to teach mankind to get a properly outlined impression of physical objects. During the cultural period of Ancient India man gradually conquered the physical world by learning the use of his physical senses. As man conquered the physical world he correspondingly lost sight of the spiritual world. The veil between the physical and the spiritual worlds got more and more impenetrable.

The various stages of this process of separation from the divine world are chronologically described on the following pages. Sympathy for the physical world constantly increased. Man had to connect himself with planet earth in order to develop self-consciousness and 'I'-awareness. The 'I' which was created by the Gods had to facilitate human freedom and independence. To reach this goal a fundamental change took place in the relation between the so-called four sheaths, or bodies, of man: the physical body, the ether body, the astral body and the neo-natal 'I'. These four sheaths used to be loosely interconnected. In the course of this development the four sheaths telescoped into one another. They got more tightly connected than before. The result was that the chakras, the senses of the soul in the astral and ether body, got less active than before. That is why clairvoyance diminished and as an inner necessity a personal memory system started to develop. Initially this occurred in the shape of external memory aids as we shall see, followed by a fully internalized memory.

Gradually man found the means to conquer the external physical world. He learnt how to become a real citizen of the earth and enjoy his daily life cut off from the spiritual world. He learnt how to live without his Gods. The physical world was no longer experienced as 'maya' but as real earthly matter. Man discovered nature forces and he invented all sorts of equipment. Consciousness of the spiritual world was completely obscured in the end, though traces of clairvoyance remained present in exceptional cases. This obscuration is penetratingly symbolized in Germanic mythology in which the rainbow bridge connecting the earth and the heavens collapses and even the Gods die in a fierce battle called Ragnarök or 'The Twilight of the Gods'. In the twenty-first century, however, there are spiritual signs noticeable to the discerning observer that the broken rainbow bridge has been restored to its former glory.

I have chosen to start this journey through the history of art with the first appearance of the rainbow some twelve thousand years ago according to the mythical story of Noah and his ark. I consider this moment to be the start of a new stage in the creation of mankind. Man seems to have woken up at that moment. His view of the world and of his own being had changed after this divine deed. From that very moment his chakras, until then more outer than inner organs, with all their revolving astral and ethereal energies were drawn inside the physical body and started to slow down—thus diminishing clairvoyance. The chakras, the senses of the soul, were more and more hampered to do their work due to this ever-increasing tangling up with the physical body. The outer rainbow with its seven colours gradually became an inner rainbow in the shape of the seven colours of the seven main chakras. The physical eyes in contrast were enabled to have a more detailed look at the physical world. They could see the outer rainbow from that moment on.

In the twenty-first century we seem to experience an entirely new phase in the development of the human phenomenon. The four sheaths of man, after centuries of continually telescoping into one another, are now gradually sliding out again, which results in an increase of a new kind of clairvoyance. The chakras, freed from being too intensely linked to the physical body, are getting a new chance to speed up their circular movements and enfold their petals, to do their work on a physical and a psychological level. The difference is that man with his newly developed 'I' can become the leader, the manager, of this impressive process. He can become his own Noah, the new captain of his own ark. This time he will not be sailing at random and hoping for a continent to land on, but he can head for a destination of his own free will, trusting his inner compass, his own seven chakras, his own inner rainbow.

Within the scope of this book it is not possible to pay attention to the development that the 'I' lives through between death and a new birth. The concept of history also applies to this intermediate period in which the 'I' travels through the spiritual world to its following incarnation. In that phase the 'I' not only processes all experiences of its previous life on earth but also gets inspired by the spiritual world, which instils new tasks and new karmic situations that will give the following life its form. The period in the spiritual world between death and a new birth is not paid attention to in the exoteric approach of history. The concept of the human phenomenon as an ever-changing historic being would be more complete if both periods, the one on earth and the one in the world of the spirit would be taken into consideration.

The discerning reader may notice that the figure of Christ is not dealt with here in a separate chapter. Although we can deduce from spiritual science and many other esoteric sources that Christ's deed on Golgotha and his resurrection are of essential importance in the development of human consciousness, I decided to touch upon this subject only briefly. The theme is so overwhelmingly extensive that a single chapter would not be sufficient. A separate book could well be filled with all that has become known about this subject over the ages. Christ, as the meaningful spirit of planet earth, may be looked upon as both the initiator and the ultimate goal of the entire development of the human 'I'.

Education is not the subject of this book. However, the parallel between the overall development of human consciousness and the development of each child on its way to adulthood must be briefly mentioned. The German biologist and philosopher Ernst Haeckel (1834–1919) postulated an advanced version of the so-called 'recapitulation theory'. The development of the individual parallels and summarizes its species' evolutionary development: 'Ontogeny recapitulates phylogeny.' In other words: while growing up a child repeats all consecutive stages that mankind experienced through the ages. This concept was taken by Rudolf Steiner when he drew up the curriculum of the Waldorf Schools in 1919. The sequence of teaching material used in Waldorf schools more or less parallels the same chronological sequence you will find in this book. All teaching material supports the child's development. Knowledge of these developmental stages of human consciousness as described in this book can help understand the developmental stages in education and vice versa.

A note on the cover: 'The Vitruvian Man' by Leonardo da Vinci is an ingenious representation of the human being as a citizen of two realms: the spiritual world, represented by the circle, and the terrestrial world, represented by the square. These two worlds are connected by the seven main chakras of the human being, each having their own colour and their own task. This seven-coloured inner rainbow bridge coincides with its archetypal mirror image of the same seven colours in the sky, when sun and rain coincide. The combination of Leonardo's Vitruvian Man and the rainbow on the cover image is intended to show the hidden relationship between mankind and the cosmos.

Prologue

The Rainbow

The rainbow as we can see it today is mentioned in several ancient documents, but it is Noah's story in Genesis, the first book of the Bible, that is best known. The story tells us that after the Flood Yaweh, Noah's God, set the rainbow in the sky as a token of his covenant with Noah promising that such a disaster would never happen again. 'I do set my bow in the cloud and it shall be for a token of a covenant between me and the earth. And it shall come to pass when I bring a cloud over the earth, that the bow shall be seen in the cloud'. (Genesis 9:13.) This momentous deed poses the question how the atmosphere of the earth would have looked like before this covenant. Apparently it was not possible for human beings to see the rainbow before this divine deed. We may derive from this that either human perception was different or the earth's atmosphere was put together in a different way. Further research leads us to Plato, the Greek philosopher, who in his *Critias* and *Timaeus* writes about Atlantis and a huge tsunami that completely flooded this continent. Rudolf Steiner describes how the air in the Atlantis period was like mist, less clear than nowadays. He also tells us that Manu, who is also mentioned in the Vedas from Ancient India, leads his people from Atlantis to drier areas in present India. These people seem to have had a dreamlike consciousness quite different from our consciousness. In Atlantis and Ancient India people are said to have been less awake by day and they seem to have slept less deep in the night than in our times. They were clairvoyant and they considered the physical earth to be 'maya', illusion. The spiritual world was seen as the real world. Agriculture and cattle breeding did not exist as such. They fed themselves with everything the earth was able to produce by itself. Their world was a real land of milk and honey. Datewise we can say that this kind of consciousness existed around 8000 years before the Christian Era. Human consciousness was a collective phenomenon then. Only the initiates, who were in touch with their Gods, gradually acquired an awareness of the physical earth as we have now. An example to illustrate this could be the fact that people in general saw the spiritual beings around a flash of lightning, but they could not see the flash itself as clear-cut as we see it now. The initiates were there to help the people train their senses and to instil interest in the physical world. Something had to change in their chakras, the senses of the soul, so that they could connect with the earth on which they lived. These seven rainbow-coloured senses, located in the astral body, had to be adapted to earthly circumstances. The earth could no longer be the floor of heaven.

Ancient India

Krishna and Arjuna

Arjuna guided by Krishna on his chariot

After the Flood, Manu and his seven Rishis organized a new society in present India. This cultural period of Ancient India lasted from 7227 until 5067 BC. All spiritual wisdom of this period was transferred orally from one generation to the next and eventually written down in the Vedas, the Upanishads and in the *Mahabharata* epic. An event from the Bhagavad Gita, which is a part of the *Mahabharata* epic, can illustrate how human consciousness developed to a different level.

In an armed conflict the famous archer Arjuna is about to shoot his lethal arrows to the enemy who in fact are his family relations. Suddenly he holds back and does not shoot. Then Krishna, the avatar of the god Vishnu and representing the future human 'I'-organization that is to be developed on earth, appears and encourages Arjuna to take up his bow and arrow and kill the enemy. Eventually Arjuna obeys and starts shooting.

Krishna instils the new power of the 'I' in Arjuna thus enabling Arjuna to distance himself from hereditary forces that are present in the blood ties that he had with his family relations and were hampering the development of his future 'I'-consciousness.

If the hereditary forces in the blood are too strong the individual human being cannot come loose from family ties and cannot really develop a personality of his own. This was a truism back then and still is in our own time. Calling your children after someone in the family can put too heavy a weight upon the shoulders of the child and is likely to block personal development.

Ancient Persia

Ahura Mazda and Zarathustra

This winged symbol found at the ruins of Persepolis is associated with the religion of Zoroastrianism, and has been commonly considered to represent Ahura Mazda

The torch of the development of human consciousness is handed on to Ancient Persia in present Iran and Iraq. This Ancient Persian cultural period lasted from 5067 until 2907 BC. Ahura Mazda was worshipped as the sun god. There is a reference in the Bible to this religion in Ezekiel 8:16–17. There we read: '(…) and they worshipped the sun toward the east'.

Several ancient texts mention Zarathustra. The name means 'gold star', as the prophet or priest of Ahura Mazda. Pliny (AD 23–79) tells that Zarathustra lived 6000 years before Plato's death, which was in 347 BC. Plutarch (AD 46–124) states that Zarathustra lived 5000 years before the Trojan War (1260–1240 BC). Aristotle tells that Zarathustra lived 6000 years before Plato's death in 347 BC. However complicated dating his life may be, from the Avesta (the holy text of Ancient Persia) it appears that a certain personality called Zarathustra had really lived. The name is probably a title used by more than one priest of the Ancient Persian religion. Zarathustra taught his people that earthly matter is an expression of the spiritual. Earthly matter is a modification of the spirit. He gets the task to lead his people to develop agriculture and to domesticate wild animals. Wheat is developed from wild grass and eating apples are cultivated from wild forms, and so on. Zarathustra taught the ancient Persians to really have a good look at the earth. The earth is not 'maya', but a place to develop a civilization. Ahura Mazda gave Zarathustra a dagger to open up the earth, to create furrows to put seeds into, and he gave him a whip to tame wild animals. By connecting with the physical earth, awareness of a counterforce grew simultaneously. The ancient Persians called this counterforce Ahriman, the opponent of Ahura Mazda. Ahriman is often described as an evil force, inimical to all human endeavour. However, this being played and still plays a crucial role in the development of human consciousness. Ahriman is the one who holds sway in the realm of physical manifestation. Without his influence no earthly matter would ever exist. All necessary hardening processes, such as the growth of our skeleton, are the effects of the ahrimanic forces which are still active. The point is that this hardening influence must be kept in check otherwise the life forces cannot make themselves manifest.

Ancient Persia

Avesta

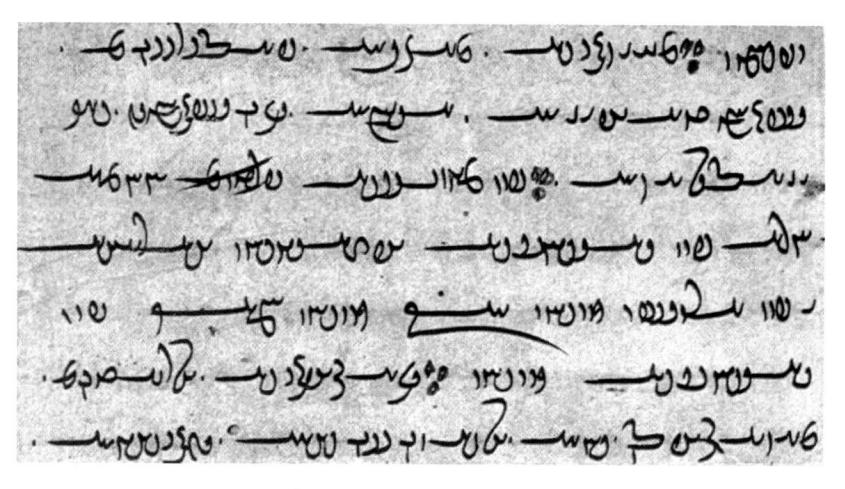

A manuscript from the Avesta. The Bodleian Library

The holy texts of Ancient Persia are known as the Avesta. After being handed down orally through the ages these texts were eventually written on cow hides. Unfortunately only a fraction of them have survived. Most were destroyed in 331 BC when Alexander the Great conquered the city of Persepolis. After looting the palace, which included a library, the whole city was burned to the ground. It took a long time before the Avesta reached Europe. In 1718 part of the Avesta was brought to the Bodleian Library in Oxford, England.

Due to the arson mentioned above, the influence of Islam at a later date, and the conquering Mongols, we now look at the ruins of an important ancient religion.

Ancient Egypt and Babylonia

Ziggurat

Partially reconstructed ziggurat at Ur, present-day Iraq

The cultural periods of Ancient India and Ancient Persia were followed by the third twin cultural period of ancient Egypt and Babylonia which lasted from 2907 till 747 BC. An example from this period to illustrate the ongoing development of human consciousness is the ziggurat.

The more people got focused on earthly matter, the less they experienced the connection with the spiritual world. Nevertheless the longing for the divine remained. In the light of this psychological make-up we can understand the building of the ziggurats, huge tower-like buildings on which priests tried to connect with their gods and their abodes in the sky. The remnants of this ziggurat, built in *c.* 2000 BC, are still standing in Ur, in Mesopotamia, present-day Iraq. It is the shrine of the moon god Nanna. Much wisdom about the stars and about organizing the calendar was developed here and afterwards transported to other parts of the world.

Ancient Egypt and Babylonia

The Tower of Babel

Pieter Brueghel the Elder (c. 1525–69), The Tower of Babel *c. 1563. Museum Boijmans Van Beuningen, Rotterdam*

The story of the Tower of Babel can be read in the Bible, in Genesis 11:4. The painter took the Colosseum in Rome as an example. Take note of the white track on the left along which buckets of slime were transported to the bricklayers at work on the top, which should eventually reach heaven. Just as the ziggurats this Tower of Babel can be understood as a landmark in the development of human consciousness. Contrary to human pursuit the connection with the divine world had to be cut off. Only then could human beings further get into touch with the earth. Yaweh, the God of the Jews, saw how the tower was built and he did not agree with this initiative. He said: '*Let us go down and there confound their language that they may not understand one another's speech*' (...) '*and they left off to build the city*' (Genesis 11:7).

The Babylonian confusion of tongues resulted in even more interest in life on earth. People had to make themselves understood. They had to develop an interest in other languages of their world.

Ancient Egypt and Babylonia

Gilgamesh

*Gilgamesh, stone relief from the palace of the Assyrian king Sargon II
c. 700 BC, Height: 6 m. The Louvre, Paris*

Gilgamesh is the central character in the *Epic of Gilgamesh*, the greatest surviving work of early Mesopotamian literature. Gilgamesh is a demigod of superhuman strength. He is King of the city of Uruk, in present-day Iraq. He ruled his country around 2600 BC. The story was written down in cuneiform on clay tablets which were kept in the library of Ashurbanipal in Nineveh, the capital of Assyria. The library was created in the seventh century BC.

One event in this epic illustrates the changing human consciousness. At a certain stage in the life of Gilgamesh a fight takes place with the Bull from Heaven. Together with his friend Enkidu Gilgamesh tries to kill this creature. Eventually the bull is killed but Enkidu also dies from his wounds. Gilgamesh wonders what strange 'sleep' has closed his friend's eyes. He talks to him and he touches his body but Enkidu does not awake any more. From this short episode we can derive that Gilgamesh is confronted with a new phenomenon: death. Before this developmental stage people were still clairvoyant to such a degree that they could follow the soul after death on its way to the spiritual worlds. Gilgamesh represents the new stage in which mankind could only stare at the body of the deceased wondering where the personality, the 'I', had gone.

It is in the same period that the Kali Yuga, as known in Indian scriptures, started. This era, also called the Dark Age, was to end around 5000 years later. According to Rudolf Steiner this happened in the year 1899 after which human beings gradually opened up again to spiritual matters.

Ancient Egypt and Babylonia

The Pyramids

Pyramids near Cairo, Egypt

Much has been written about the Egyptian pyramids. These impressive structures have never failed to impress all who saw them for the first time. Nothing seems to be certain about the use of these carefully built structures. There are suggestions that these structures served as a means to enable the soul of the deceased to travel through a special shaft in the pyramid to a certain part of the zodiac. The deceased pharaoh for example was enabled to travel in that way to the star sign of Orion or, more specifically, to the star Sirius which was considered to be the dwelling place of the Egyptian god Osiris.

In general it can be said that the Egyptians wrestled with the disappearance of a clear connection with the divine world. This appears also from the fact that at a certain stage the pharaoh, supposedly the initiated godlike ruler, did not understand his own dreams any more. In the Bible we can read about Joseph who is called from prison to explain the dream the pharaoh had about the seven fat cows and the seven lean cows. After the explanation the pharaoh elevates Joseph to viceroy of Egypt. (Genesis 41: 1–45.)

In ancient Egypt people developed the art of measuring the land after it was flooded by the Nile. In that way they understood how to divide and till the fertile soil. The external world was more and more conquered in that way.

Ancient Egypt and Babylonia

The Obelisk

An obelisk at Karnak, near Luxor

The obelisk is sometimes called a petrified sunbeam. This is quite understandable when we realize that the sun was worshipped as a god: Amon-Re. Through the obelisk the god touched the earth. The top is in fact a pyramid high up in the sky which was often covered with gold. The texts in hieroglyphs tell about the pharaoh who then reigned over the country and about the sun god. As people had not yet developed an inward personalized memory system they were reminded in this way of important events much in the same way as we place statues in our towns to commemorate events or people.

The upright position also expresses the budding awareness of the slowly awakening 'I'. The force of the 'I' that erects the physical body and aligns the seven chakras into a perpendicular line was felt more and more and was expressed in the perfectly perpendicular obelisk that was not attached to the earth but was kept in place by its own weight.

Ancient Egypt and Babylonia

The Erected Stone

A group of erected stones in the Negev Desert, near Eilat, Israel

One of the oldest recordings of erecting a stone to commemorate an important event can be found in the Bible, in Genesis 28:18. When Jacob awakes from his dream he says: '*Surely the Lord is in this place (...). This is none other but the house of God and this is the gate of heaven. And Jacob rose up early in the morning and took the stone that he had put for his pillow and set it up for a pillar and poured oil upon the top of it.*' After clairvoyance got more and more blurred, the need for a memory system became clearer.

Putting up stones can be interpreted as attempts to replace clairvoyant reading in the ethereal Akashic Chronicle by physical memory aids.

Ancient Egypt and Babylonia

Tutankhamun

Gold mask of pharaoh Tutankhamun's mummy, c. 1323 BC. Egyptian Museum, Cairo

Ancient Egypt fulfilled a crucial task in the process of making the human soul interested in all things connected with the earth. The price to be paid for this inescapable process was the cutting off from the world of the Gods. Mankind got more and more interested in earthly matters due to which his day consciousness increased and at night he was faster asleep than ever before. As clairvoyance diminished, memory capabilities had to be developed. Human beings could no longer spontaneously get in touch with the world of the ether in which all events are recorded. This ethereal memory system is also called the Akashic Record. Rudolf Steiner was able to clairvoyantly 'read' in this 'book' and tell his audience about events that took place long ago.

The development of a personal memory was started. Mummification of the dead was one of the means to arouse interest for the physical earth. The soul of the deceased stayed longer with the mummified body than when the body was not prepared in this way. The initiated priests tried to get in touch with the soul that was still hovering around the body. In that way they managed to get information from the spiritual world.

By having been mummified the soul of the deceased was given a chance to have an intense and prolonged look at his or her own body. This experience made such an impression on the soul that in the next incarnation the soul was even more focused on earthly matters, which led to modern materialism. With the help of Egyptian mummification mankind has learnt to love the physical earth.

Ancient Egypt and Babylonia

David

Gian Lorenzo Bernini (1598–1680), David *Borghese Museum, Rome*

The story of David defeating Goliath can be found in the Bible in 1 Samuel 17. This sculpture represents David about to throw a stone with his sling at his gigantic opponent Goliath. David hits Goliath right between the eyes. The stone hits the spot where the sixth chakra can be found, which is the chakra that plays an important part in clairvoyant perception. This story can be construed as an act aiming to kill clairvoyance, which was necessary to enable mankind to further develop a firm connection with the physical world. David serves here as a metaphor for this necessary change. It is also a striking feature that David is the smaller and Goliath the bigger character in this story. The same occurs in the story of Odysseus (Ulysses) deriding Polyphemus (see page 31). Whenever two characters play a role in a metaphoric story, the smaller one represents the power of the brain, the power of logical thinking, whereas the bigger one represents the power of metabolic processes located in the lower part of the body.

Even if we take for granted that this event took place in historical, physical reality, we can also observe a second layer in this event. 'As above, so below', is an adage of ancient times that draws attention to at least two levels of reality that occur simultaneously.

Ancient Greece

The Golden Bough

Joseph Mallord William Turner (1775–1851), The Golden Bough *(1834). National Gallery, London*

Moving on to the next stage in the development of human consciousness we arrive at ancient Greece. Clairvoyance had further decreased. The phenomenon of death really posed a problem for the people of ancient Greece. Man had connected himself even more with the physical world, which he grew to love more and more intensely. The ancient Greek had a certain knowledge of the world in which man arrived after his death through his mythology, which in fact was a memorized narrative of clairvoyantly acquired impressions. This world, which was not understood, was considered to be very unpleasant. 'Better to be a beggar in the upper world than a king in the realm of the shades' is a well-known saying typifying the general mood in ancient Greece. Nevertheless we read in Virgil's *Aeneid* about the hero of the Trojan War, Aeneas, how he wants to consult his deceased father in Hades, the realm of the shades.

In the painting we see the Sibyl, a priestess of Apollo, in front of the gateway to the underworld. Aeneas is allowed access to the underworld if he cuts a golden bough from a holy tree. He travels through the underworld guided by a Sibyl, who carries the Golden Bough, which spreads some light in this dark world. The story is said to have taken place in Cumae, in Italy, not far from Naples. The scene illustrates that there was a longing in ancient Greece to get in touch with the deceased and that it was extremely difficult to establish such a contact.

Ancient Greece

Ulysses and the Cyclops

Joseph Mallord William Turner, Ulysses Deriding Polyphemus *(1829). National Gallery, London*

A good example of the disappearance of clairvoyance can be found in this picture. This disappearance did not happen by chance. It was a developmental stage orchestrated by the creating forces that are at work behind the scenes. In Greek mythology this important stage is represented in the adventures of Ulysses.

In the picture we see the moment at which Ulysses escapes from the cave of Polyphemus, the cyclops who had captured him. While in the cave Ulysses had put a tree trunk in the fire until the end was red hot. With all his power Ulysses drives this trunk right into the cyclops's only eye, thus blinding him. Hanging from the belly of a sheep Ulysses manages to escape. He arrives on his ship where he is welcomed by his mates.

We see the creatures from the water, the undines, leading the ship to safer waters. In the background, close to the horizon, we see Apollo the sun god, in his chariot, taking the sun to a resplendent sunrise. Metaphorically speaking we can say that not only a new day is about to start but a whole new era is heralded. Turner knew how to value this important scene in the development of human consciousness.

The eye of the cyclops symbolizes man's third eye, the sixth chakra, located in the middle of the forehead between the eyes. Clairvoyance had to stop so that the vision of the other two eyes could further develop. Apollo can also be seen as the Sublime Charioteer symbolizing man's future 'I- power' which will eventually rule human life on earth instead of a divine being.

Ancient Greece

The Minotaur

Floor mosaic in a Roman villa, Switzerland, c. AD 200

The myth of the Minotaur, who lived in the centre of a mazelike labyrinth under the palace of King Minos (*c.* 2200 BC) in Knossos on the island of Crete, can shed some light on the progress of man's budding faculty of thought. This faculty, at the height of its development in ancient Greece, made possible the mathematics of Pythagoras and Euclid, and the philosophic ideas of Socrates, Plato and Aristotle among others. When Theseus arrives and is about to enter the labyrinth to find and kill the Minotaur, who has the body of a man, the head of a bull and feeds on human beings, the daughter of King Minos, Ariadne, gives Theseus a ball of string which he is advised to unroll while finding his way through the labyrinth. After having killed the monster, Theseus would be able to easily find his way back again—which is what happened.

In this myth the difference between a labyrinth and a maze seems not to be as clear-cut as we understand these concepts today.

Essential to the Minotaur myth is the fact that Theseus uses the string that was given to him to find the exit. This string may be looked upon as the 'thread' of logical thinking that will lead to the right solution of a problem. The windings of the labyrinth represent the windings of the brain.

The myth seems to highlight the increased capacity of brain power. In ancient Greece man seems to be abandoned by the gods but he seems to be given, though in a budding form, the power of thought. When he seems to have got lost in the world of sense impressions, the liberating power of his own Theseus, his 'I'-consciousness, defeats the monster and leads him back to the physical world which he then sees on a different level.

Ancient Greece

King Aegeus at Delphi

King Aegeus consults the Pythia seated on a tripod. Dish by the Kodros Painter, c. 440 BC. Museum of Antiquities, Berlin

The legendary King Aegeus of Athens remained childless, which posed a problem as to his succession. He travelled to Delphi to consult the Pythia, the priestess sitting on a tripod. In the picture painted on a dish we see King Aegeus and the Pythia who is staring in a dish. She is about to reveal her message to Aegeus. The enigmatic message was: 'Do not loosen the bulging mouth of the wine skin until you have reached the height of Athens.' On his return

Aegeus cannot do anything other than think about the meaning of this puzzling oracular utterance. The continuation of this story is beyond the scope of this book, but something more can be said about the phenomenon of the Delphic oracle.

The Delphic oracle had the task to educate and further develop the human power of thought. By posing all these riddles, the solution of which was of extreme value, the people involved were pressed to mobilize all possible powers of thought to come up with a solution. 'Practice makes perfect' was also applicable to the progress of human thinking.

Before the heyday of the oracles we see that the directions given to Odysseus, for example, mainly came from the gods as we can read in Homer's *Odyssey* (see p. 28). Odysseus' power of thought was still young. The gods were still necessary to lead him. These directions were pretty straightforward and not oracular at all. Odysseus, for instance, was told in detail how he had to get hold of the hair of Kirke, the sorceress. Odysseus, representing the changing human consciousness of mankind, only gradually mastered the power of thought.

Ancient Greece

Achilles Tries to Kill Agamemnon

Giovanni Battista Tiepolo (1696–1770), The Rage of Achilles.
Villa Valmarana, Vicenza, Italy

In the *Iliad* we can read about a conflict between two warriors in the Trojan War, Achilles and Agamemnon. At a certain stage a duel is about to begin between these two. At the very start, just when Achilles lifts his sword to deliver a lethal blow, Pallas Athena, the goddess of wisdom, checks his anger and stays his hand. The duel is prevented in that way.

This event shows how the power of reasoning still is in divine hands. Quite different is the way in which Odysseus stays his anger when he has eventually arrived home and is hit by a footstool that is thrown at him by one his wife's lovers. Odysseus locks his anger in his heart. He does so by his own power of reason.

As a result of all his adventures, which represent the developmental stages of the human soul, Odysseus is able to incorporate this relatively new capacity in his psychological make-up. Individualized human thought is taking the lead. The gods gradually withdraw their leadership. Mankind is on its way to independence.

Ancient Greece

Olympia

Running track of Olympia, Greece, c. 350 BC

The ancient Olympic Games in Greece were religious and athletic festivals started in 776 BC and held every four years at the sanctuary of Zeus in Olympia. Foot races on a track of 185 m (600 Greek feet) were part of the games.

Right from the start in 776 BC the names of the winners were listed. These winners were admired and immortalized in poems and statues. These personal victories gave an important boost to the awareness of the slowly awakening 'I' consciousness. That is why the ancient Olympic Games represent a new stage in the history of human consciousness. The 'I' once again was enabled through these activities to get a firmer grip on the other sheaths of man: on the astral body, the ether body and the physical body.

The effect of a personal victory is still felt in modern man. At times we all need what is called an ego-booster. This feeling was completely new at the start of the ancient Olympic games.

Ancient Greece

Plato's Cave

The Greek philosopher Plato (427–347 BC) described in *The Republic* the human condition on earth in his well-known allegory of the cave. We human beings are chained to a wall in a cave. Also we cannot turn our heads, as they are fixed. We are facing a blank wall on which all sorts of shadows are projected by things that are passing along a fire burning behind us. Watching these shadows is as close as we can come to reality. The task of the philosopher, who is able to watch the complete scene, is to explain the human situation to these closed-in human beings.

The description is related to Plato's theory of forms or ideas. This world of invisible ideas, represented by the shapes and forms that are passing along the fire, is the real world according to Plato.

Plato's allegory has ultimately and sadly led to an uncompromising kind of dualism: there are two worlds, a visible, physical world and a world of invisible ideas. This split can still be found in present-day science. It is a direct result from the fact that clairvoyance had almost completely stopped in ancient Greece and man wondered how he could understand his surrounding world.

Fortunately opinions seem to change gradually in our days. Earthly substances, in whatever shape, are more and more looked upon as spiritual processes that have come to rest. Plato's ideas are the ethereal casting patterns, casting moulds, ethereal matrices, in which spiritual realities materialize. They are organizing basic principles giving shape to our visible world. A snow crystal, for example, got its form from this invisible world. When it melts the form disappears into the ether again. A fresh light is cast upon the way in which we look at earthly matter. A wonderful unification takes place of spirit and matter as soon as we accept this way of thinking.

Ancient Greece and Rome

The Mission of Wine

Caravaggio (1571–1610), Bacchus, *god of wine (c. 1594).*
Uffizi Gallery, Florence

In the development of human consciousness alcohol played an important role. In the Bible, in Genesis 9:20, 21 we read: 'And Noah began to be a husbandman and he planted a vineyard and he drank of the wine and was drunken and he was uncovered in his tent.' Noah seems to have been the first who experienced the power of alcohol. The use of alcohol was intensified and came to a climax in ancient Greece. Dionysus, who was called Bacchus by the Romans, was the Greek God of wine and all its effects upon the human being.

In anthroposophy alcohol is looked upon as having been an aid for the human 'I' to further find its way into the physical body. The 'I' as the fourth sheath of man had to develop a stronger grip upon the other three sheaths: the astral body, the ether body and the physical body. Thus the 'I' continued its descent from the world of the spirit down to the earth. When alcohol is used the four sheaths initially loosen up, get less united. After alcohol is used, however, the four sheaths telescope together in a more firm way than ever before. This condition cannot be undone. After having used alcohol for many years the four sheaths are intensely interlocked. This condition closes off the world of the spirit. Man has indeed become a creature that can only be aware of earthly circumstances. And what is more, the faculty of memory has also been influenced by the use of alcohol. When it is said that we seek oblivion in alcohol we mean that we start forgetting things. The depths of memory are obscured according to Rudolf Steiner even to such a degree that man started to forget the whole process of reincarnation, which was widely known in previous cultural periods. Previous lives were obliterated from memory, which enhanced the feeling of having just one life on earth in the here and now. This all was necessary in the development of mankind in order to completely 'land' on earth.

Rudolf Steiner tells about the wedding at Cana as described in the Bible in the Gospel of St John where water, usually looked upon as a holy substance, was turned into wine. 'As the era of Christianity drew near, man was destined to enter upon an epoch of concentration upon earthly efforts. (...) The knowledge of incarnation, therefore, was to be lost for two thousand years and wine was the means to this end.'[*]

As to the use of alcohol in our own age, Rudolf Steiner tells us that whoever tries to get in touch with the spiritual world through spiritual science had better not use alcohol for it shuts down the way to this world—it closes the 'doors of perception', a phrase used by Aldous Huxley. Anybody who meditates or does spiritual exercises will notice the harmful effects of alcohol. Clairvoyance should come

---

[*] Rudolf Steiner, *The Gospel of St John* (GA 94, Lecture 7).

back in a new way which means that the newly developed 'I' is lord and master of the process. Alcohol will annihilate what is acquired by meditation. According to an anecdote Rudolf Steiner answered a lady who could not accept the harmful effects of wine in this sense with the following words: 'It has the same effect as if you would build up a house by day and pull it down at night'.*

---

*Herbert Hahn, *Begegnungen mit Rudolf Steiner* (Meetings with Rudolf Steiner).

Ancient Greece and Rome

Metre and Memory Systems

Scene from The Persians *by the Greek dramatist Aeschylus (525–456 BC)*

In the spoken as well as in the choral parts of ancient Greek drama a variety of metres were used. Greek metre is based on patterns of long and short syllables creating a rhythm. These patterns are the fundamental building blocks of Greek verse. Rhythm is an important memorizing device. The development of memory systems forms an integral part of the development of human consciousness. As clairvoyance decreased, other ways had to be found to access events from the past. External objects can be used as reminders such as statues, wall paintings, etc. As soon as these are seen once again the event related to it leaps to mind.

See more on the development of memory aids below. A well-known example of the development of a memory system is told by Cicero (106–43 BC) in his *De Oratore*. The Greek poet Simonides of Ceos was once invited to a banquet. At a certain moment he was called to come outside because there were two visitors who wanted to see him. After he had left the building the dining hall roof collapsed killing all guests and leaving him unhurt. Later on he is invited to identify the victims, who were completely crushed. He manages to do so by bringing back to mind where the guests had been seated at the table. This event prompted Simonides to develop the 'memory method of loci'. The arrangement of localities preserved the actual facts in the memory of the poet.

The ancient Greeks can be seen as the inventors of the art of memory, which was subsequently passed on to ancient Rome in their oratory tradition and further to the general European tradition of the stage. In the centuries before the invention of book printing the art of memory was of vital importance. Mnemosyne is

Two Finnish rune singers reciting a cycle of ancient songs from memory

the mother of the Muses and the personification of memory according to the ancient Greeks, and in that sense of utmost importance in the creative processes of all arts.*

Through all ages up to the present day rhythm has always been a great aid in memorizing drama or poetry texts. When the old photograph above was taken, the tradition of Finnish rune singing had almost died out. The songs—runes—recounted mythical heroic deeds in the form of epic poetry orally handed down from ancient times. The verses were sung by two singers simultaneously, so that conformity to the right words was guaranteed. The singers' memory was supported by the movement of their bodies in the rhythm of the poetry lines. The singing might be accompanied by someone playing the kantele, a string instrument like a harp.

The 'rune songs' might have eventually become lost, but early in the nineteenth century a country doctor, Elias Lönnrot, collected and wrote them down. His published arrangement of the verses (1835 and 1849) constitute what has become known as the Kalevala epic. Although Lönnrot edited the material and even added some lines of his own, most of it is either a word for word rendering of the original runes or at least fairly close.

---

*The whole subject of the development of memory systems through the ages is extensively dealt with in Frances Yates's *The Art of Memory* (1966).

Ancient Rome

The Colosseum

The Colosseum in Rome

The construction of the Colosseum was finished in AD 80. It is one of the greatest works of Roman architecture and engineering and also the largest elliptical amphitheatre in the world. It has become the iconic symbol of imperial Rome. Fifty thousand spectators could find a seat to watch the performances. In hot weather a huge awning was spanned as a circular roof to protect the audience from being burnt by the sun.

Religion in ancient Rome was an amalgamation of indigenous and imported religions which played in important role in everyday life. The towns were dotted with a whole variety of temples and altars. Even an altar for the 'unknown god' could be found. However, the creative powers of the Romans were more directed to mastering all sorts of technical problems than to worshipping living gods. They cut down all trees in the area round Cumae, the Apollo sanctuary near Naples, for example, to get wood for shipbuilding. No god showed his wrath.

The disappearance of the gods culminated in the erection of the colossal statue of the Emperor Nero (AD 37–68) commissioned by himself. This bronze statue was 30 metres in height and was located in his imperial villa complex in Rome. After Nero's death the statue was modified by his successors into the likeness of Helios, or Apollo, the sun god. A sun-ray crown was placed on the head to equate the Emperor with this divine being. Nero's head was replaced several times with the heads of succeeding emperors.

After the birth of Christ the influence of the human 'I' grew stronger and stronger in ancient Rome, thus effectively quenching general clairvoyance. The concept of the 'testament' was introduced. The word is derived from *testa*, the word in vulgar Latin denoting 'head'. This meant that for the first time man was seen as an individual with his own identity in civil law.

Ancient Rome

St Augustine

Benozzo Gozzoli (1420–97), St Augustine reading the Epistle of St Paul.
*Scene from a fresco cycle on the wall in the Apsidal Chapel of the
Sant'Agostino Church in San Gimignano, Italy*

When St Augustine of Hippo (354–430) visited Ambrose (339–97), bishop of Milan in 386, he saw Ambrose bent over a book, apparently reading without moving his lips. St Augustine did not understand what was going on. He could not believe that Ambrose was reading without producing the sounds of the words.

Augustine tells us about this experience in his *Confessions*.

Somewhat later the monks around Augustine are surprised to see Augustine read in silence. He had clearly mastered the process. Apparently reading in silence, as we all do now, was a relatively new phenomenon in the fourth century. In the history of human consciousness this stage is another landmark indicating how consciousness further developed into this inner, strictly individualized capacity.

When teaching young children nowadays how to read we come across the same stage. Initially the whole class reads a text aloud, like a choral chant. Only gradually does the individual pupil develop the ability to read without sound. In the transitional process we see that children do not produce sound as such but merely move their lips. Once again we come to realize that every human being on his way to adulthood repeats the stages that mankind as a whole has experienced on its way to the present level of consciousness.

Germanic Mythology

Yggdrasil

Yggdrasil is an immense mythological ash tree mentioned in the old Norse *Edda*, a literary work compiled in the thirteenth century from earlier and traditional sources by Snorri Sturluson (Iceland, 1179–1241). This metaphoric tree with all its inhabitants shows the way in which the ancient Germanic tribes of northern Europe saw the whole of creation. The world of the gods was located in the top of the tree. The underworld was found in the region of the roots and between these two worlds Midgard, our earth as we know it, could be found. The Bifröst Bridge, also called the Rainbow Bridge, guarded by Heimdall, connected Midgard with the world of the gods.

The stories from the age-old *Edda* shed a specific light on the development of human consciousness. Especially the section called Ragnarök, which describes the death of the gods, deserves extra attention in this context.

The god Balder is one of the first who dies. Balder represents the clairvoyant capabilities of man. He is killed by an arrow shot by his blind brother Hoder who represents our everyday consciousness, which is blind to the events that take place in the ether world. The more powerful everyday consciousness gets, the less clairvoyant man becomes. Mankind is separated from the divine world by the death of Balder. Incidentally, the same process takes place in the life of every child during its growth to adulthood.

During the frightening struggle of Ragnarök the gods perish. Richard Wagner (1813–83) composed an impressive set of four operas, *Der Ring des Nibelungen*, of which *Der Götterdämmerung (Twilight of the Gods)* is the fourth and last part.

The Bifröst Bridge collapses during Ragnarök, and man's connection with the divine world is broken off.

The story ends less sorrowfully than expected. There are Lif and Lifthrasir, who represent future mankind. They had managed to hide in the trunk of Yggdrasil during the fierce battle of the gods. They survived the disaster. Life on earth, though profoundly altered, continues according to this impressive Germanic myth.

The death of the gods, this Ragnarök, can be understood as the inability of mankind to actually see the gods any longer. The gods did not really die—they withdrew from human perception. This stage in the development of human consciousness had to come about for the creation of a new kind of man that could survive entirely trusting his own consciousness as his rational compass, independently from the gods.

The ancient myths and legends of northern Europe wonderfully show how human consciousness developed. These stories and their embedded wisdom deserve more attention than they are usually given.

The Middle Ages

Chartres

Labyrinth on the floor of Chartres Cathedral, c. 1220

The labyrinth on the floor of the cathedral in Chartres in France poses all sorts of unanswered questions. It might be considered as representing a pilgrim's progress on his way to meet his inner self or to meet Christ. Just as the labyrinth from the Minotaur myth (see p. 33), it may also be looked upon as a representation of the human brain as the ultimate point of application for the 'I'-activity in the physical body.

A slightly different shape, the spiral staircase, with all its turns and bends, is another metaphor of the power of the brain. A good example is the spiral staircase as described in Grimm's fairy tale of the Sleeping Beauty. At the age of 14 the Sleeping Beauty discovers, in her own palace, a spiral staircase which she had never seen before. It is at that particular age that the power of reason, of the brain, really starts to develop. At the top of the spiral staircase the Sleeping Beauty discovers an old woman at a spinning wheel. The Sleeping Beauty has a go, pricks her finger and falls asleep—the power of reason has arrived and the senses do not see the world of the spirit any more.

In Rembrandt's painting *The Philosopher*, of a later date, we also see this age-old archetype of the winding staircase. In the light of the subject matter of the painting we may assume that in this case the human power of thought with which the philosopher keeps himself busy is represented by this image of the winding stairs. The silent language of symbols adds to the power of this beautiful painting.

Rembrandt (1606–69), The Philosopher *(1633). Louvre, Paris*

Early Renaissance

Mont Ventoux

Mont Ventoux, France

In a letter to his confessor, Petrarch (1304–74), the Italian scholar and poet, describes his journey to the top of Mont Ventoux in the south of France. There seems to be no other reason for this trip other than to reach the top and see what the view would be. Half-way an old man strongly advises Petrarch not to go any further because it is of no use. He had done it himself and after this nobody had ever tried it again. Yet Petrarch continues his journey and climbs to the top. When he arrives at the top Petrarch is overcome by a strange feeling of loneliness. He takes from his pocket a little volume of St Augustine's *Confessions* and starts reading.

Here, on the top of Mont Ventoux, two worlds meet: on the one hand the world of the Middle Ages in the shape of the closed-in soul reading a sacred text and, on the other hand, we see the start of the

Renaissance, in which an individual opens up to a new world view with literally far-reaching vistas.

This scene on Mont Ventoux has led to defining Petrarch as the first modern tourist. To be able to clearly observe the surrounding world, as tourists do, we must be able to objectify this outer world. If we remain an integrated part of it we will never be able to consciously experience our own situation.

This process is beautifully described by William Wordsworth (1770–1850) in his poem *Intimations of Immortality*. He says that 'heaven lies about us in our infancy' but that the 'shades of the prison house begin to close upon the growing boy'. And a bit further down: 'The youth, who daily further from the East must travel, still is Nature's priest', but in the end this light-filled world

Petrarch

must be left behind and it will 'fade into the light of common day'.

We are sent out of Paradise to get fully aware of ourselves and about the surrounding earthly circumstances. Here again we see that the history of human consciousness is repeated in the process of growing up.

Early Renaissance

Perspective

Giotto Bondone (1266–1337) The Marriage at Cana.
Cappella degli Scrovegni, Padua

Giotto is considered to be the first painter of the Italian Renaissance. Giorgio Vasari describes Giotto as making a decisive break with the prevalent style of his time. He drew accurately from life itself. The picture here shows how the phenomenon of perspective is realized. The canopy under which the twelve apostles are seated can be seen from the front as well as from underneath. The angles of the wall create a closed-in space. The table is depicted in perspective and the plates on the table are given an elliptical shape as is right seen in this position.

Although in previous centuries long before Giotto a budding representation of perspective can be seen in works of art, on the walls of Pompeii for instance, Giotto's attempt to create an image with a certain depth in a flat surface is rather successful. The representation of perspective is further developed in the following centuries. Human consciousness seems to experience once again a new developmental stage at the start of the early Italian Renaissance. The surrounding physical world is looked upon in an entirely fresh way. The human brain suddenly seems to be able to really look round objects thus placing them in a new three-dimensional perspective. In this exciting voyage of discovery, of how perspective can be represented on a canvas, the name of Brunelleschi must be mentioned as well.

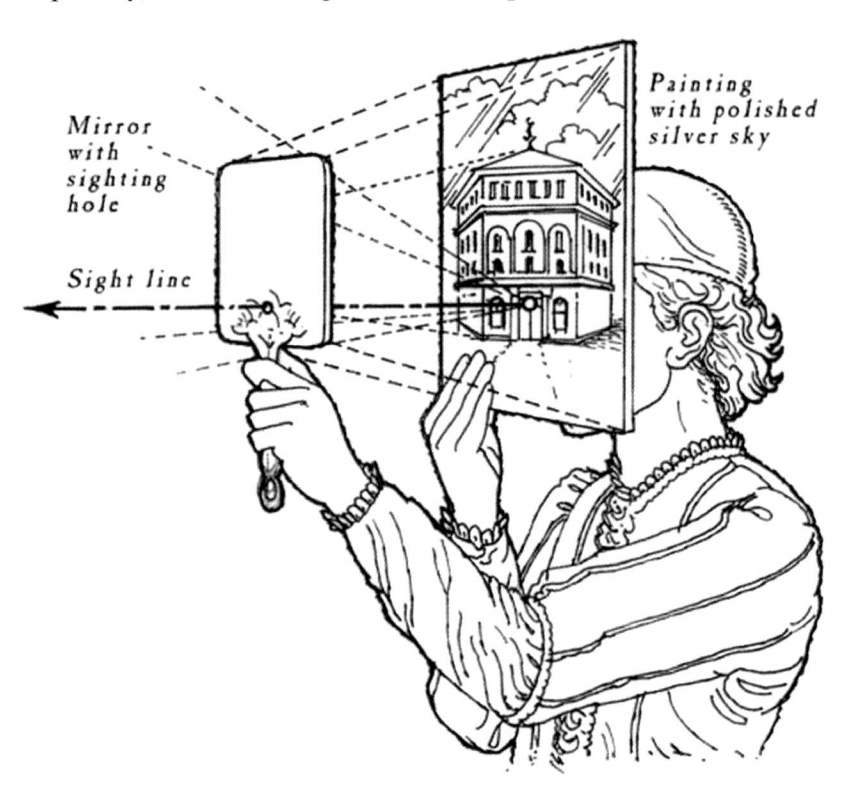

A device was designed by Filippo Brunelleschi (1377–1446) to obtain the correct geometrical linear perspective to be used in a drawing of the Baptistery in Florence, Italy. The viewer, facing the Baptistery, looked through a hole in a panel. A mirror was then placed in his view resulting in an image similar to the actual view of the Baptistery. The reflection in the mirror taught artists how to paint images not as flat, two-dimensional forms but as three-dimensional structures. Linear perspective spread across Europe as a new artistic tool since then.

Correspondingly, children round the age of ten are inclined to ask their teacher for some assistance when they try to draw, for example, a road that should fade away at the horizon or a house that should really represent an actual situation. The teacher will then teach his pupils how the laws of perspective work. As soon as they master these laws the pupils invariably start drawing everything in perspective for a certain period of time until the novelty has worn off. In follow-up lessons two-point and three-point linear perspectives can be introduced. Children repeat all stages that humanity has gone through over the previous centuries.

From the discovery of perspective onwards painters digressed more and more from the stylized figures of medieval art. A more naturalistic style took the upper hand.

Piero della Francesca (1420–92), The Ideal City *(1470). National Gallery, Urbino, Italy. In this picture representing the rules of architecture and town planning the laws of perspective are faultlessly shown*

Sixteenth century
Memory Theatre

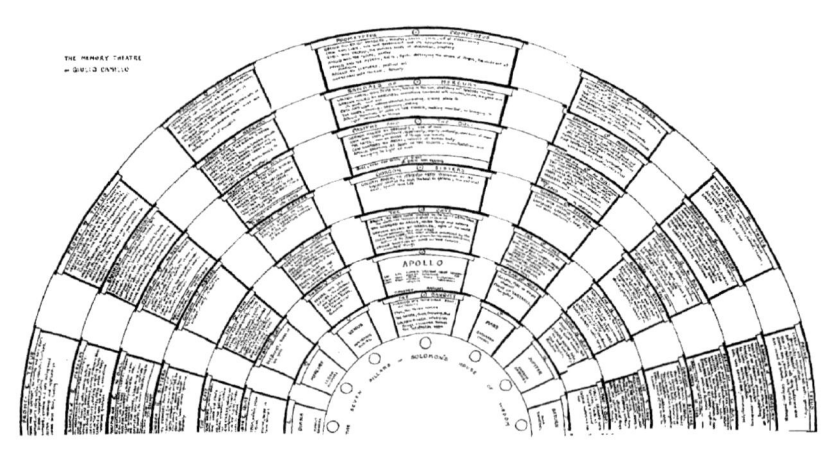

Reconstruction of the memory theatre of the Italian philosopher Giulio Camillo (1480–1544)

The development of human consciousness is closely and inevitably related to the development of individual memory. The 'I'-consciousness largely depends on memory. Without memory the 'I' would completely disappear and become a nonentity. Memory and the 'I' are fellow travellers along the road of the ever-changing human consciousness. We have seen (pp. 46–7) how external objects, rhythm and location can be important means for promoting memory.

The memory theatre is a Renaissance extension of localized memory as described previously. Giulio Camillo described 'the theatre of memory' in his *L'Idea del Theatro*. It is concerned with the eternal aspects of all things. Giulio writes about a system that turns scholars into spectators. The whole of creation unfolds in a theatre-like setting. Conceptual relationships are given shape in a spatial representation of chronology. The concept may be looked upon as a mind map. It refers to the idea that for instance actors in a play remember their lines according to the spot they are standing on.

In Giulio's memory theatre all that is known to mankind is given a place on the various rings of the amphitheatre. The shape is inspired by the seven pillars of wisdom as mentioned in the Bible (Proverbs 9:1): 'Wisdom has builded her house. She hath hewn out her seven pillars...'

The imaginary visitor to the theatre standing in the orchestra pit gets a complete overview of all available knowledge.

The representation above remarkably resembles one half of a gleaming CD disk, our present-day icon of memory.

Sixteenth century

Copernicus

Nicolaus Copernicus (1473–1543), Polish Renaissance mathematician and astronomer, who formulated a heliocentric model of the universe in his On the Revolutions of the Celestial Spheres, *published just before his death in 1543.*

Legend has it that Copernicus was presented with the first copy of his book on his deathbed. The manuscript had already been finished in 1532 but he had refused to publish the text. He had feared the scorn to which he would expose himself on account of the incomprehensibility of his ideas. Copernicus' new concept of the universe was supported by Galileo Galilei (1564–1642) who, due to his use of the telescope, could confirm what Copernicus was actually saying. In 1633 Galileo was suspected of heresy for following the theses of Copernicus. Copernicus' book was placed on the Index, the list of forbidden books drawn up by the Roman Catholic Church. Only in 1835 was the book dropped from the Index.

The Copernican revolution can be understood as a paradigm shift from the Ptolemaic model of the universe, in which the earth was thought to be the centre, to the Copernican one, in which the sun is seen as the centre of the solar system.

As appears from the dates mentioned above it took many years before this paradigm shift was generally accepted. This shift is defined by the fact that since the sixteenth century we human beings have been able to observe the universe from every angle, from every location. We do not need the earth any longer as a special position. This shift in observational possibilities is an important developmental step in human thought.

Copernicus told us *not* to trust our senses when we look up at the sky. Our newly developed power of thought presented us with quite a different image from what we thought we saw. Mankind was able to really objectify his surroundings a step further. This step can be seen as the starting point of the seventeenth-century scientific revolution. We can only study a certain object when we have sufficiently distanced ourselves from it.

Sixteenth century

Hans Holbein

Hans Holbein the Younger (1497–1543), The Ambassadors *(1533).*
National Gallery, London

This painting looks very realistic, but every object has a symbolic meaning. Holbein was commissioned to produce this painting on the occasion of the meeting of two friends : the French Ambassador to England, Jean de Dinteville (left), and the young bishop Georges de Selve (right). On top of a kind of table we see all sorts of instruments used to study the stars and measure time. On the lower shelf our attention is drawn to more earthly pursuits such as music, mathematics and geography.

The most enigmatic symbol is at the front of the painting. It can only be identified when one stands at the right of the painting close to the wall. The symbol turns out to be a skull, symbolizing death and a warning not to place too much faith in luxury objects. The skull has been distorted from a perspective point of view, a technique that is known as anamorphosis, to make the enigma of death even more ominous.

However, when we have a very close look we can discover an even more disguised symbol. In the left-hand top corner the discerning eye can see a crucifix, partly hidden behind the green curtain. And this is the reason why this painting has been incorporated in this book. It mirrors the spiritual situation of the age. Religion, the Christian faith, has been banned from life in general. Science and personal affluence have taken its place. From a spiritual point of view we can say that man has almost completely landed on earth— almost, because the enigma of death is still there and often comes unbidden. The number of people who believed in life after death and turned to Christ for comfort was getting smaller and smaller in those days.

Sixteenth-century religion is adumbrated by looming rationalism and all its positive and negative effects.

Seventeenth century

Rembrandt

Rembrandt van Rijn (1606–69), Self-portrait (1629). Mauritshuis, The Hague, Holland

The Dutch painter Rembrandt is a unique painter in the development of art. Rudolf Steiner calls him the first painter of the consciousness soul, which typifies the fifth post-Atlantic cultural period (1413–1573).

Rembrandt represents the new psychological make-up of the seventeenth century, especially in his many self-portraits—he produced over 90. Rembrandt manages to express a subtle harmony between soul life and outward appearance. Through intense and continuous observation of the reflected image of his own face, Rembrandt acquired a high degree of self-knowledge. He was able to do so because he knew how to objectify the surrounding physical world on the one hand and on the other hand he knew how to simultaneously penetrate into the spiritual sources of human life. He does not observe reality as was done before, but he approaches objects as a real outsider. He even used a perspective screen as a gadget to get perspective in his paintings, in order to enhance a sense of reality. By doing so he shows individual freedom and real observation in contrast to representing inner life as such.

Rembrandt demonstrates a high degree of originality. He never

Rembrandt, Tobias Healing his Blind Father *(1636). Staatsgalerie, Stuttgart, Germany*

travelled to southern Europe to study nature or Italian art, for instance. He studied the Bible for all his biblical scenes. He read Latin and Greek. His interpretation was his own. Rembrandt knew that colour is born between light and dark, just as Goethe would show later on. In Rembrandt's work the source of light, which in fact creates the whole image, has always an unexpected and even enigmatical ring—it is never accidental.

At the end of a lecture on Rembrandt on 28 November 1916 in Dornach, Switzerland, Rudolf Steiner tells us that the artist's engravings are of essential importance to get to know the real Rembrandt. Rembrandt's surrender to this form of art belongs to 'the movement that Rembrandt wanted to introduce into the world'. We may wonder which movement was hinted at by Steiner. The little rose on the floor in one of Rembrandt's most famous paintings, *The Night Watch*, is by some interpreted as a secret hint that Rembrandt was well informed about the Rosicrucian movement that sprung up at the start of the seventeenth century. Rembrandt may have been inspired by this so-called Rosicrucian enlightenment, which probably also taught him the secrets of chiaroscuro painting.

The scene above is taken from the apocryphal book of Tobit. Old Tobit has been blinded by bird droppings that fell into his eyes while he was sitting in front of his house. In the book we further read about Tobias, Tobit's son, who is sent by his father to a distant relative to collect some money he had lent. Tobias is accompanied by someone called Azarias. When they are on their way Tobias is attacked by a huge fish. Azarias tells Tobias to kill the fish and to take out heart, liver and gall which he does. With the heart and the liver Tobias performs miraculous healings while being amidst his distant family. Back home Tobias applies the gall from the fish to his father's blind eyes upon which Tobit is instantaneously cured and gets back his eyesight. At the same moment Azarias turns out to be the Archangel Raphael who in disguise had protected and advised Tobias all along. This final scene is depicted by Rembrandt in this painting. The painting can be considered as a pictorial meditation on the miracle of vision. Such a meditation can lead to the following thoughts.

Rembrandt was well aware of the secrets of light and darkness and he was well informed about the Christian content of the Bible, the apocryphal book of Tobit included. In the story the fish from which the healing organs are taken may be construed as a symbol of Christ, the Ichthus. Traditionally Raphael is connected with all curative aspects of the Spirit, of Christ in this context. In this pictorial meditation several things happen at the same time on different levels. The power of Christ, through this symbol of the fish, heals and restores Tobit's eyesight.

Rembrandt presents this ancient story to highlight this curative power of Christ. As a seventeenth-century painter he also seems to tell that a new era has started in his own lifetime. The age of the consciousness soul has definitively begun in which there will be new developments in science and in politics. New vistas are opened up, new light is shed on life in the seventeenth century and far beyond.

Seventeenth century

Still-Life Painting

Pieter Claesz (c. 1597–1661), Still Life *(1627)*

A still life is a respresentation of inanimate things such as furniture, utensils, fruit, dead animals, dead flowers, hourglasses, etc. The Dutch diplomat and scientist Constantijn Huygens (1596–1687) was probably the first who in 1630 used the phrase 'inanimatis' when referring to this type of painting. Still-life painting, as part of settings, is found in ancient Egyptian tombs, in Roman wall painting in Pompeii and in religious pictures and portraits. But the revival in the seventeenth century takes a new turn. It emerges as a distinct genre in western Europe. Not only are these paintings decoration as used to be the case, they are full of symbols, many a time referring to the transience of life. As can be seen in this picture, the candle of life has nearly reached its end, the spectacles refer to the reader in his old age, the book of life has almost been read, the glass has almost been emptied and the snuffers are ready for use. This genre of still-life painting is called 'vanitas' for obvious reasons. There are many more sub-genres of still-life painting but in all cases the painter, and the observer as well, is able to distance himself from the depicted scene. The physical world is objectivated to a maximum degree. Neither the artist nor the looker-on is part of the scene. This type of observation 'from the outside' is highly characteristic for this stage in the development of human consciousness.

After the development of the sentient soul in the ancient Egyptian-Babylonian cultural period, and the development of the intellectual soul in the ancient Greek-Roman period, the consciousness soul made itself manifest in the period called the Renaissance and finds a representation in still-life painting.

Seventeenth century

Isaac Newton

Isaac Newton and his apple tree as depicted in Punch *magazine*

The lines of Alexander Pope (1688–1744) on Isaac Newton (1642–1727) aptly highlight and summarize Newton's life: 'Nature and nature's laws lay hid in night, but God said: Let Newton be and there was light.'

Newton's contributions to mathematics, dynamics, celestial mechanics, astronomy, optics, natural philosophy and cosmology are of essential importance to the development of science. He was president of the erudite Royal Society, and was knighted in 1705.

But he was also dedicated to—and this is less known—theology, biblical chronology, prophecy and alchemy. In that context Newton was related to the Cambridge Platonists, a group of Anglican divines closely connected to Cambridge University in Newton's lifetime. This being a scholar of two seemingly different and separated worlds became very clear when in 1936 Newton's library was brought to auction. There were over 170 books dedicated to the Rosicrucians, cabbala and alchemy in this collection. John Maynard Keynes (1883–1946), economist, patron of the arts and member of the literary circle the Bloomsbury Group, said about Newton after this auction: 'He was not the first representative of the Age of Reason, he was the last of the Magi'. And this statement exactly summarizes the transition that took place in the seventeenth century. Modern science as we know it now was still in its infancy and at the same time magic and all that that implied occurred widely.

In this context, although taking place 23 years before Newton was born, the three visions or dreams of René Descartes (1596–1650), the French mathematician and philosopher, can be mentioned. Although a major figure in seventeenth-century rationalism, Descartes attached much value to three visions he had on 10 November 1619. In these visions a divine spirit revealed to him a new philosophy from which Descartes concluded that the pursuit of science would be for him the pursuit of true wisdom. Another remarkable event took place in 1623 when Descartes made a pilgrimage, as a part of his wider travels, to Loreto in Italy. He went there to see the house of the Holy Family that was miraculously taken away by angels from Nazareth. It landed finally in Loreto according to tradition. Descartes seems to have been a more naively religious soul than we usually think he was.

In whatever way Descartes's views and beliefs may be construed, remarkable it remains, and that is why he is mentioned here, that these visions and this pilgrimage, irrational as they were, were taken so seriously by the dubbed father of rationalism.

Eighteenth century

A Scientific Experiment

Joseph Wright of Derby (1734–97), An Experiment on a Bird in the Air Pump *(1768). National Gallery, London*

Joseph Wright of Derby can be looked upon as the first professional painter who expressed the spirit of the Industrial Revolution. He widely made use of the chiaroscuro effect, emphasizing the contrast between light and darkness in the candle-lit spaces in which scientific experiments took place. His paintings about the birth of science are mainly based on the meetings of the Lunar Society of Birmingham, which took place between 1765 and 1813. During these meetings a group of influential English scientists, industrialists and intellectuals met and exchanged all sorts of relevant knowledge. During the meetings investigations were conducted into scientific subjects such as electricity, geology and meteorology. The society was also subject to the struggle of science against religious dogmas upheld by the church in the Age of Enlightenment.

In this painting we see that a bird can neither fly nor breathe when the air is removed from the bowl by a pump. Air, though invisible, is a natural phenomenon to be reckoned with. It supports life and in this case also the movements of the bird's wings. The experiment is watched by people from various age groups. All generations seem to be present.

The painting has a metaphorical aspect as well. The expressions on the various faces may refer to the concern over the possible inhumanity of the coming age of science.

Eighteenth century

Coalbrookdale by Night

Philip James de Loutherbourg (1740–1812) Coalbrookdale by Night.
Science Museum, London

This painting is a famous image of the changing landscape caused by the Industrial Revolution. The blast furnaces and iron works became a tourist attraction especially at night. The scene evoked awe and national pride at the same time. The painting also has an infernal quality. The scene with heroic, hard-working figures is lit by the yellow glare of the fire and by the moon.

The English Romantic poet Anna Seward (1747–1808) mourns the flight of nature spirits, such as the wood nymphs and sylphs, from their rightful realm in the following warning lines:

> *Now we view their fragrant and their silent reign*
> *Usurpt by Cyclops—hear, in mingled tones*
> *Shout their throng'd barge, their pond'rous engines clang*
> *Through thy coy dales, while red the countless fires*
> *With umber'd flames, bicker on all thy hills*

Before the age of painters such as Joseph Wright of Derby and Philip James de Loutherbourg, these technical scenes were not considered suitable to be painted, to be transformed into works of art. People seem to have developed a certain pride in all these experiments and discoveries resulting in an entirely new look.

Experiments as the one with the bird and the air pump were taken more and more seriously, even to such a degree that these were linked by opponents to one of the causes of the French Revolution in which Reason was upheld as a new Gospel. Scientists were blamed for all upheaval caused by the Revolution and the French scientist Antoine Lavoisier (1743–94) even ended his life under the guillotine.

Edmund Burke (1729–97), the English politician and philosopher, wrote in 1796 in his 'Letter to a Noble Lord' that the radicals of the Revolution considered men no more than they do mice in an air pump. Wright's painting of the bird in the air pump, done 20 years before, seems to have had a forecasting ring.

Eighteenth century

Robinson Crusoe

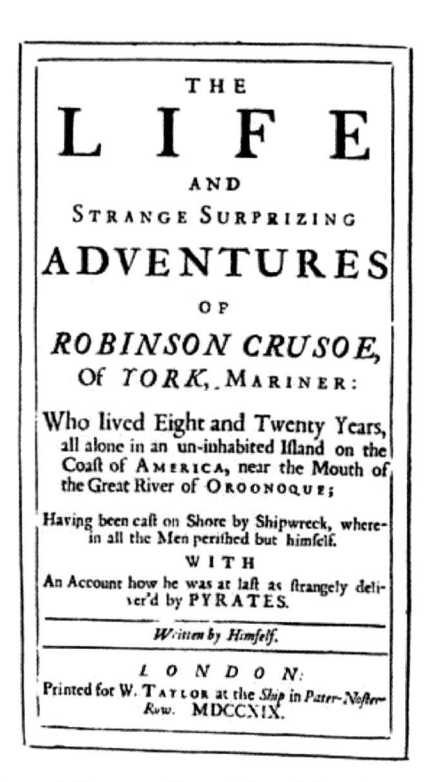

Daniel Defoe (1660–1731), The Life and Strange Surprizing Adventures of Robinson Crusoe of York, Mariner, *written by himself, London, MDCCXIX*

Not only in the pictorial arts but also in literature the ongoing change of human consciousness is clearly reflected. At the start of the eighteenth century collective traditional sources used by authors are gradually replaced by individual experiences as subjects for their writing activities. Plots were not taken any more from mythology, history, legends, fables, as was done before. Eventually the so-called link-and-frame stories were no longer necessary to convince the readers that the present story was handed over to the author from a certain, real-life spokesman. Former authors accepted the general conditions of life because they thought that these conditions were static and given by God. Due to Rationalism all this had changed. Life used to be lived by eternal values, but from then on life was lived by real time.

The rise of the English novel reflects this new approach. The word 'novel' refers to a new kind of book, a new category. *Robinson Crusoe*, written by Daniel Defoe, is looked upon as the first English novel. Other examples of this new genre of a slightly later date are *Moll Flanders*, also by Daniel Defoe, published in 1722, and *Tom Jones*, written by Henry Fielding in 1749.

The new way of writing can be summarized in the following way. The content of a novel is purely fictitious, though there might be a vague source of inspiration from actual facts. Formal realism is the defining phrase. The characters all have family names, not just a first name. The location in which the story is placed is described as real. The reading public act as a kind of jury—they wish to know as many real details as possible. In that sense the novel corresponds with another novelty: the newspaper. Pamphlets had been spread in all times but now well-organized distributors of news appeared. *The Tatler* was published in 1709 and *The Spectator* in 1711.

The phrase 'the willing suspension of disbelief' coined by Samuel Taylor Coleridge (1772–1834) in 1817 refers to the wish of the readers that subject matter in the end must be related to reality, however impossible the story seems to be. The audience is expected to suspend judgement concerning the implausibility of the narrative. And they could and did so.

Technical progress such as the improvement of indoor lighting by gas lamps and the development of all sorts of machinery resulting in more leisure time also enabled people to read more than they used to do. After 1750 this individualizing process is also reflected in the appearance of names on shop signs instead of symbols.

In the context of the ever-changing human consciousness in literature the concept of 'stream of consciousness' must be mentioned as well. The phrase was used by William James in his *Principles of Psychology* (1890) to characterize the unbroken flow of thought and awareness in the waking mind. Sense perceptions mingle with conscious and half-conscious thoughts, memories, feelings and random associations. The reader is allowed to get unhampered and unlimited insight into the character's mind, which apparently could not be described by authors and could not be understood or accepted by readers in previous centuries. Famous first examples of the refined stream of consciousness technique can be found in James Joyce's *Ulysses* (1922) and Virginia Woolf's *Mrs. Dalloway* (1925).

Eighteenth century

The Feast of Reason

The Procession of the Goddess of Reason, *1793, by Etienne Béricourt*

In this painting we see Mademoiselle Maillard, probably a dancer, singer or prostitute, festively carried on a float into the Notre-Dame at Paris as Goddess of Reason. She took her seat on a throne in front of a temple dedicated to 'Philosophy' which was erected on a platform in the middle of the choir by order of the Municipality of Paris on 10 November 1793. Some busts of famous philosophers, such as Voltaire and Rousseau, were placed on either side of the entrance.

The caption of the image of the temple tells us that we are in the month named Brumaire, the month of fog. This new name referred to the period of October/November in the second year of the French Republic. Rationalism or reason was hailed as the one and only saviour of mankind. Even time and space were measured in a new, rational way from then on. The decimal system was introduced, and eventually in many parts of Europe.

Much has been said about the French Revolution. Most striking in my view is the positivity at the outset in contrast to all the negativity at the end of the turmoil. Many scholars agree that the slogan Liberty (in cultural life), Equality (in political life) and Fraternity (in economic life) could have caused the start of a new era. The ideals were also propagated by the astonishingly obscure Comte de Saint Germain (1710–84) who tried to awaken in the French people awareness of an impending new social order. Rudolf Steiner says of him: 'The Count of Saint Germain has been the exotic reincarnation of Christian Rosenkreutz in the eighteenth century' (said in *The Mission of Christian Rosenkreutz*, lecture of 27 September 1911, GA 130).

Through this statement Steiner creates a link with the historical Rosicrucians of the seventeenth century. The attempt by these Rosicrucians to change society at the beginning of the seventeenth century when Europe was also at war has a certain similarity with the turmoil in the second half of the eighteenth century. Both attempts failed to create a lasting change.

When asked about Napoleon's contribution to the French uprising, Rudolf Steiner answers that Napoleon has forgotten his task with which he had come to earth. The only thing Napoleon managed to do was, Steiner continues, introducing a stream of ancient Egyptian pharaoh-dom with which he tyrannized Europe.

Rudolf Steiner also points at Goethe's fairy tale *The Green Snake and the Beautiful Lily*, originally published in 1795. In this

Painting by David Newbatt showing a scene from Goethe's fairy tale The Green Snake and the Beautiful Lily: *The bridge finally connects the two banks of the river, and the underground temple has risen to the surface for all to see*

fairy tale Goethe shows in imaginative pictures the way in which a human soul could become whole and free. Most impressive at the end of the tale is the imaginative picture of the underground temple that rises to the surface of the earth and becomes visible to everyone. This image indicates that all esoteric knowledge should come out into the open. There are no secrets any more concerning initiation into whatever secret lore. Goethe's fairy tale exactly represents the spiritual situation around 1800. This revelatory attempt of the spiritual world unfortunately failed to be successful.

In this context the sonnet by the English Romantic poet John Keats (1795–1821) in which he speaks about 'great spirits that now on earth are sojourning' must be mentioned. Keats, like most adherents of the Romantic movement, seems to have envisaged new infinite horizons as to the further development of mankind under the aegis of the spirit.

The whole enterprise, however, collapsed at Waterloo in 1815.

The map of Europe was redesigned and the industrial revolution progressed at full throttle. The spirit, whichever spirit this had been, had for the moment failed to radically change society. It had to wait for another chance.

Eighteenth century

William Blake

William Blake (1757–1827), Front page of The Marriage of Heaven and Hell *(1793)*

The English author and engraver William Blake claims in his *The Marriage of Heaven and Hell* that man does not consist of the duality of soul (= reason) and body (= evil) but that 'Man has no body distinct from his Soul (...) Energy is the only Life and is from the Body (...) Energy is Eternal Light.' Only very gradually we, living in the twenty-first century and with the help of all our electronic equipment, are getting a first notion of what human energy comprises. Blake seems to have known more than could be understood in his own lifetime.

A well-known quote from the same book is the following:

> *If the Doors of Perception were cleansed every thing would appear to man as it is, Infinite.*
> *For man has closed himself up, till he sees all things thro' narrow chinks of his cavern.*

These lines perfectly illustrate the psychological make-up of the people of those days. The power of human thought, otherwise known as rationalism, had completely taken over, held sway in the realm of mankind. Few had an inkling, or inspiration, of how the spirit of the age was ardently trying to make itself felt. Blake, Goethe, the Count of Saint Germain, Wordsworth and Keats were just some of them.

Blake's statement about the Doors of Perception is still of great value to us who are living in the twenty-first century. Our image of the world and of mankind depends on the input we get through our senses. If this image is blurred we only get partial information. Waldorf education aims at training all our senses, which are twelve in number. If we add to these twelve sense the seven main chakras—our inner rainbow—as senses of the soul, we can imagine how important it is to get all our Doors of Perception wide open so that all relevant information can get unhampered access.

Modern Times
Rudolf Steiner

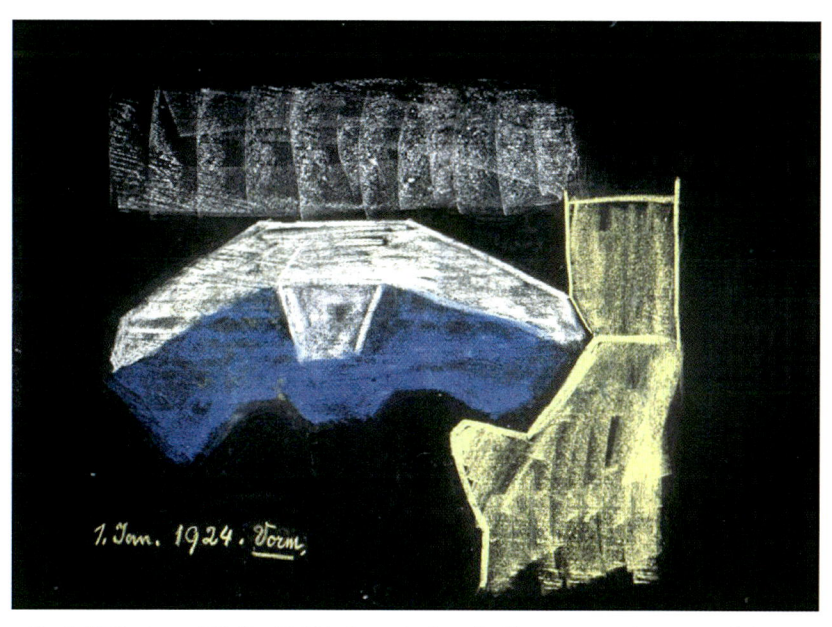

Rudolf Steiner (1863–1925), board sketch illustrating shapes and forms in architecture

In a book about the history of human consciousness Rudolf Steiner must certainly be mentioned. This clairvoyant initiate, philosopher and man of science knew a thing or two about this ongoing process. In his *World History in the Light of Anthroposophy*, a series of lectures given in December 1923 in Dornach, Switzerland, he demonstrates in what way human consciousness kept on changing through the ages. His many examples from all these consecutive cultural periods never fail to stimulate the reader of these lectures to further investigate the matter. The book you are reading now is a direct result of these revealing and interesting examples Rudolf Steiner has given.

After having studied Rudolf Steiner's anthroposophy for many years, I get the impression that the spiritual world once again is trying to make itself manifest in the physical world through Rudolf

Steiner's contribution. The Kali Yuga, the Dark Age in Hinduism, ended after five thousand years in 1899, after which the light of the spirit got another chance to clear up all darkness in the human mind. Steiner and all who worked with him at the time and all who are trying to further develop his contributions in all fields of work seem to be co-workers of the spirits of the light.

A century has passed since Steiner's life on earth. Honesty compels us to say that only fragments of his inspiration have materialized after this relatively long time span. Yet his many attempts to pave the way to the spiritual world and his enormous energy are still felt by many people who have opened up to spiritual matters. Everything Steiner has said about the seven main chakras is of immense value today. He pointed out that the chakras have not always been as they are now and that they will even further develop. The result of this change will be that man will again be able to observe the world of the spirit, but not led on by the Gods but under the guidance of his own higher self, his 'I'.

Time will tell whether Steiner's unignorable contribution to the development of human consciousness will last and will be taken further into the following centuries.

Modern Times

Heralds of the World Wide Web

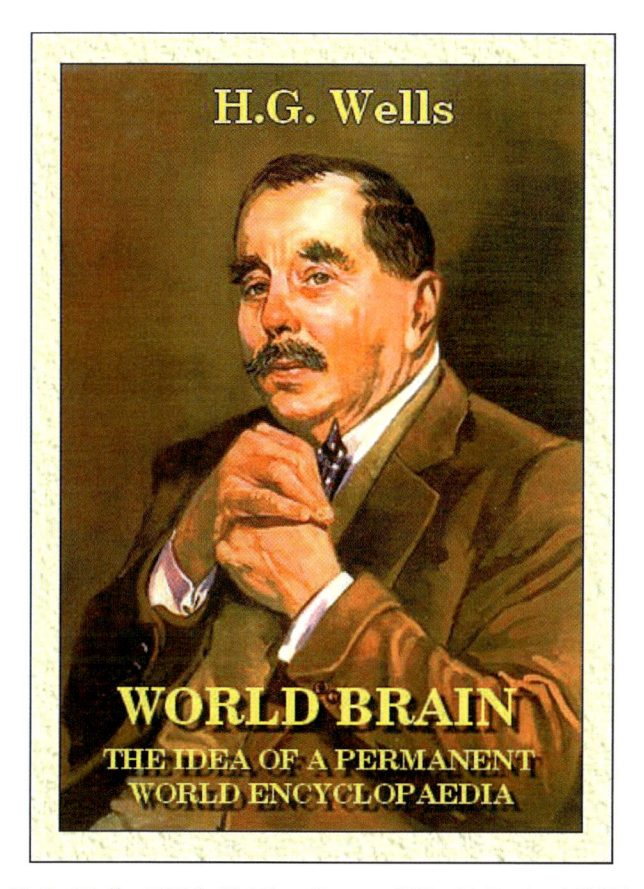

H.G. Wells (1866–1946)—Cover of World Brain *(1938)*

In his publications the English author H.G. Wells gave many warnings about the dangerous new powers of science—with the First World War fresh in his memory and the Second World War looming. He stated that the present encyclopedias were still in the coach-and-horse phase of development. He was in favour of using microfilm to record anything and everything to make the best use of all information resources as a contribution to world peace. 'We do not want dictators, we do not want oligarchic parties or class rule. We want a widespread word intelligence conscious of itself.'

In a series of addresses and essays, collected in *World Brain*, H.G. Wells tried to convince his audience of the need of such a worldwide coming together of all available knowledge. If we just change 'microfilm' into 'computer files' it is amazing how accurate Wells's prophecy was.

The concept of a collection of all knowledge available on earth is

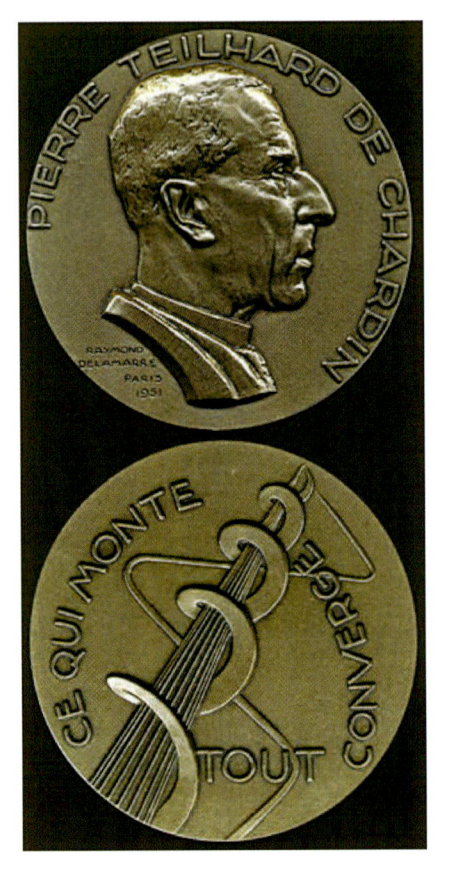

Medal carved by Raymond de la Marre, Paris, 1951, to commemorate Pierre Teilhard de Chardin. The wording 'Tout ce qui monte converge' ('All that goes up converges') refers to Teilhard's conviction that all development on earth converges to one point in the future. This point is called 'Omega'. The development started at point Alpha in the distant past. In Teilhard's view this point Omega coincides with Christ, the Spirit of planet Earth

also present in the philosophy of Pierre Teilhard de Chardin (1881–1955). This layer of knowledge around the earth he called the 'noosphere'. The concept, introduced in 1922, is that of the interaction of all human minds which grows in step with the overall progress of humanity. All human knowledge is growing towards greater integration and unification, eventually ending in the Omega Point, as Teilhard de Chardin calls the apex of human consciousness. This terminology falls in with the words of Jesus Christ: 'I am Alpha and Omega, the beginning and the end, the first and the last' (Revelation 22:13).

The World Wide Web is heralded in the works of these two remarkable visionaries.

Twentieth century

The First Argonne Computer

The AVIDAC was Argonne's first digital computer built by Argonnés Physics Division (1953), Chicago, USA

Just before World War II the development of what we now call a computer is said to have begun. The incredibly inventive human brain had discovered how to speed up calculations and how to store information in cleverly designed equipment. Initially computers needed whole rooms because of their enormous size whereas modern laptops can be taken everywhere.

The ever-improving computer technology caused a real revolution in human behaviour and the end of this tumultuous change is not yet in sight. Within the scope of this book about the development of human consciousness some lines dedicated to this huge leap should not be lacking.

From a spiritual point of view we may wonder from where these extremely intelligent IT technicians get their inspiration. A straightforward answer is not available yet. Another question is how this way of thinking structures the brain. From modern neurology we know that thoughts wire the brain. The brain has a certain plasticity. Learning how to read, for example, wires the brain, changes the brain in a way. All incoming information changes the way in which we use our brain. Information technology deeply infects and restructures the neurological circuits not only of the technicians that are working in that field but also of those who use computerized equipment every day. All cleverness, all discernment, all intelligence, stored in IT, finds its way into the brain of those who use this equipment. I am not speaking about content but about the way this content enters the brain while using computerized equipment.

The question arises whether other inspirational thoughts on completely different wavelengths will still be able to reach the brain. For instance, the so-called morphogenetic fields described by Rupert Sheldrake can be perceived by the human brain if the brain is attuned to this very sophisticated energy. Also energy as present in the aura of living beings can be noticed by finely attuned humans. In that sense the brain is like a radio that can be attuned to any sender.

It would be great to learn how to work the channel selector, the tuning knob, of our own built-in wireless set so that we can listen to the programmes of our own choice and not just pick up the programmes others want us to. After all, human beings are meant to further develop into entirely free creatures.

Modern Times

The *Sputnik*

The first Sputnik

Sputnik 1, the first artificial satellite, was launched into an elliptical earth orbit on 4 October 1957 by the Soviet Union. In two months the satellite made 1400 orbits round the earth. The satellite was a polished metal sphere, 55 cm in diameter, with four radio antennae. It was polished to make it visible from the earth.

Due to all new and valuable information provided by the sputnik, new political, military, technological and scientific developments were ushered in. And what was most interesting, man had found a standpoint outside the earth's atmosphere to observe our planet. Man had broken loose from all earthly limitations for the first time in history.

I clearly remember my own reaction to the news of the launch of the Sputnik, which in my language was called a *kunstmaan*, in

English an 'artificial moon'. I was 13 years of age and I did not feel at ease when I heard this word for the first time. I had the feeling that man had passed an ethical borderline and was now competing with the Gods. It is quite useful to call back this remarkable feeling because it brings back the world view most people had in those days. The last reminiscences about the God from my childhood who lived somewhere out there, over the rainbow, as I had seen in this wonderful film *Green Pastures*, were forcefully blown from my mind.

The Space Age had begun. In a way mankind was necessarily and unavoidably expelled from Paradise once again on his way to become a free creature that would ultimately be able to act without the interference of the Gods.

Modern Times

Google

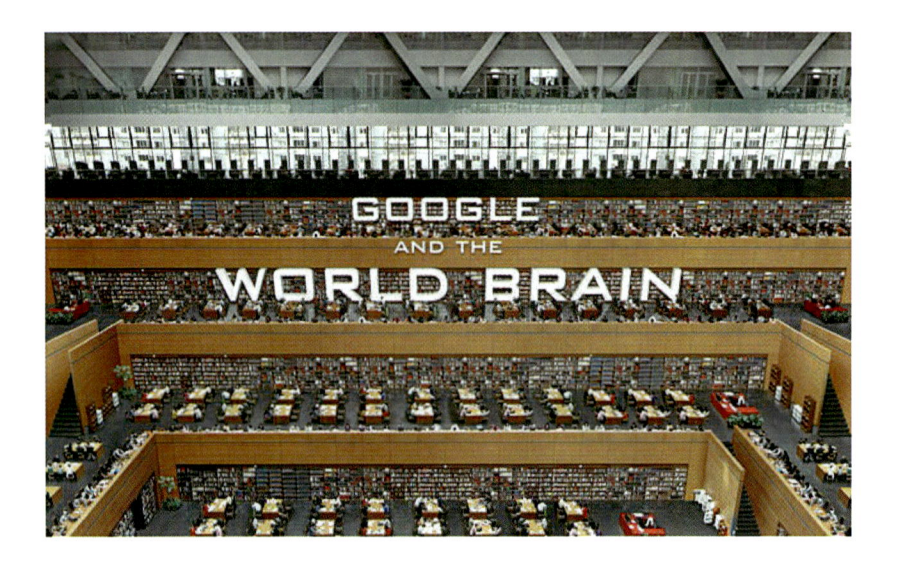

Some years ago the search giant Google started its plan to scan all books in the world. This utopian plan was forecast by H.G. Wells in his collection of essays *World Brain* published in 1938. However, authors and publishers across the world resisted Google's actions. It triggered an ongoing lawsuit because of copyrights. Already 20 million books had been scanned when the project was stopped in 2011 because of these legal problems. A film about the project released in 2013 fanned the flames even more. Some call the project an insidious and scary plot for data domination in order to improve Google's artificial intelligence projects. H.G. Wells in his *World Brain* also warned against the possible domination of those who had acquired all this information.

If Google, or someone else, ever manages to complete the project, and it must be going on ad infinitum because new books are likely to be published every day, a complete planetary memory for all mankind would come into being.

The whole concept makes me think of the Akasha Chronicle, the spiritual chronicle in which all events ever experienced by mankind and by our planet, yes, even by the universe as we know it, are recorded. And here we arrive at a bifurcation of the ways in which we can educate and train our senses. Which way is opted for?

If our senses are trained in a purely rational way in which mere brain-power is used, man will certainly manage to fulfil this World Brain project. However, if in addition to this brain-power project our seven chakras, as our personal rainbow bridge, are trained as senses of the soul *as well*, entirely different vistas will be opened up. Other sensory perceptions will become available. Other senses than our physical eyes that read letters in books will become active and this will lead us to a spiritual reality in which unfathomable horizons are bound to be revealed.

The first of the Leading Thoughts given by Rudolf Steiner can lead the way: *Anthroposophy is a path of knowledge to guide the Spiritual in the human being to the spiritual in the universe.*

Epilogue

Earth

*The weaving essence of the Light
rays forth through realms of space
to fill the world with Being.*

Rudolf Steiner, from *Verses and Meditations*

When thinking about the coming of age of human consciousness a childhood memory leaps to mind. I must have been four years old when I was taken down by my mother from our flat on the first floor to the garden below that was owned by a neighbour. When standing among the flowers and some shrubs my mother pointed upwards and said: 'Look, there is the balcony of our flat on which you were playing a minute ago.' I could not believe my eyes. I not only saw our balcony, but I saw the whole building with many balconies at the same time. Our flat appeared to be not the only one in the world. It was not the centre of life, neither a castle nor a safe haven as I had thought it was because it was spared in the war—the war in which I was born and which I had heard spoken of so often. The image gets blurred here and in fact ends. When I relive this moment, and I often do, it gives me the feeling that I then and there had fallen from paradise in which all was light, all was good, all was safe. At that moment my horizon was suddenly and irreversibly widened, be it only as far as the garden of the house in which I was born. But the lifelong process had started. The exciting journey of distancing myself from the surrounding physical world had begun. The process of developing an independent 'I', independent from my parents, independent from my family, independent from my childhood God, had made an impressive start.

As I take for granted that every human being repeats the successive developmental stages of mankind as a whole on its own way to adulthood, I tentatively use this childhood memory to get a further understanding of the psychological make-up of preceding cultural periods as described in this book. The cultural period of Ancient India as we have come to know it through the Vedas and through Rudolf Steiner's lectures seems to have the same characteristics as the developmental stage of a very young child in our present day. The comparison, of course, is not watertight in every respect, but it may help to understand how people experienced life in those distant days.

In this book I have tried to show how human consciousness has developed over the many centuries. The process of 'getting expelled from Paradise' started in a veiled past. In the ensuing stages man was enabled to further objectify his surrounding world with a burgeoning 'I'-consciousness. At the same time, as his clairvoyance diminished, his memory capacity increased. Gradually man distanced himself from the divine world from which he had come.

In the twenty-first century man has eventually placed himself outside his natural surroundings, outside nature, outside his family ties. He has become a really self-governing independent individual locked up in his body, which he mainly identifies with. The spirit was abolished by the Roman Catholic Church in AD 869 at the Council of Constantinople and even the soul seems now to play a subservient role sometimes. The physical body with all its mechanical and chemical processes seems to be our only support, our one and only reality.

When in 1969 man landed on the moon, the maximum distance between man and earth had been realized and all kinds of technical equipment launched into space provided mankind with brand new viewpoints to observe and investigate his own position in the universe. Now the time has come to realize that all acquired precious knowledge must be employed to continue man's development into a creature that knows how to make use of not only his body and his soul but above all his spirit. The next step after having completed the development described in this book must be a conscious connection with the world of the spirit, with the higher 'self' or higher 'I'. Only then will the higher 'I' be able to gradually transform the three lower sheaths, the astral body, the ether body and the physical body into the future Spirit Self, the Life Spirit and Spirit Man. Then the fourfold image of man has completely been spiritualized, which is the ultimate goal of human life on earth.

The outer rainbow given to Noah after the Flood was internalized into the seven main chakras as an inner rainbow. As soon as man gets to understand how these chakras work, how they mediate between the physical and the spiritual world, he will experience a magical feeling of wholeness. There are many ways in which we can heal our chakras if we really want to. Some details of our life will probably need to change, but every effort will pay off straight away. Let awareness of the development of human consciousness as described in this book be the start of this change. Much has been published about this specific subject and browsing the internet will provide you with many possibilities to take you further. Human beings are meant to change constantly. This metamorphic process goes on and on and defines the human phenomenon. Only when we adapt ourselves, change ourselves in time, can we enjoy the magic tour to the future.

The seven colours of the rainbow, the seven days of the week, the seven chakras and the seven notes of the octave, these are all expressions of the same spiritual world that lies at our feet and invites us in. Come walk with me, let's cross the newly restored Rainbow Bridge and be whole.

Sevenfold
Spirit-Light
pours

into me
bountiful
strengthening
quickening

Rudolf Steiner, from *Verses and Meditations*

Further Reading

By Rudolf Steiner:

The Evolution of Consciousness, Rudolf Steiner Press, 2006
World History in the Light of Anthroposophy, Rudolf Steiner Press, 1997
Ancient Myths and the New Isis Mystery, SteinerBooks, 1994
The Christ Impulse and the Development of Ego Consciousness, Anthroposophic Press, 1976
Egyptian Myths and Mysteries, SteinerBooks, 1971
Occult Science, An Outline, Rudolf Steiner Press, 2013
The Study of Man, Rudolf Steiner Press, 2004

Other authors:

Alexander M.D. Eben: *Proof of Heaven*, Lennart Sane Agency, 2012
Hunt, Valerie V: *Infinite Mind*, Malibu Publishing Co., 1989
Judith, Anodea: *Eastern Body, Western Mind*, Celestia Arts Publication, 1996
Jung, C.G.: *Man and his Symbols*, Aldus Books, 1964
Lommel, Pim van: *Endless Consciousness*, Harper Collins, 2010
Lowndes, Florin: *Enlivening the Chakra of the Heart*, Sophia Books, 1998
Meyer, Rudolf: *The Wisdom of Fairy Tales*, Floris Books, 1996
Montfoort, Joop van: *All is One*, Author-House, 2010
Oort, Henk van: *Anthroposophy A-Z, A Glossary of Terms*, Sophia Books, 2011
   Anthroposophy, A Concise Introduction, Temple Lodge Publishing, 2008
Wilkinson, Roy: *The Interpretation of Fairy Tales*, Rudolf Steiner College Press, 1984
Yates, Frances A.: *The Rosicrucian Enlightenment*, Routledge, 1972
Zajonc, Arthur: *Catching the Light, The Entwined History of Light and Mind*, OUP, 1993
   Meditation as Contemplative Inquiry, Lindisfarne Books, 2009